# HOW TO BECOME WIZARD:

*by*

**Giuseppe Giovenco**

Hi, my name is **Giuseppe Giovenco,**

and I'm the author of this practical guide of how to cook pizza at home.

I lead professional training lessons for anyone who wishes to become a pizza maker; and professional updating lessons for pizza makers that want to improve in their profession.

I invested much in my preparation in Italy, and I continue doing it regularly, to offer to my learners and clients more advanced

techniques and notions that let obtain the best results about Italian pizza.

Until now, by my lessons, I've formed a great number of pizza makers of both genders and of different nationalities, that in this moment are cooking delicious pizzas around the world.

In this part that you're going to read I give you notions to make you quickly become a pizza wizard at home and to avoid every disadvantage... I guarantee you a perfect result.

**Look out:**

This method is the result of my personal experience.

If you have food intolerances, consult your doctor.

If you're allergic to gluten, so you are celiac, don't prepare this recipe because it contains gluten.

Use an efficient equipment!

# Summary:

# Welcome!

Hello, thanks for being here; we have the same passion, isn't it?

A passion that stars with a P and ends with an A ?

A passion that smells of tomato, mozzarella and basil?

Great, you're in the right place !

Before we start, I give you a nice information...

Cooking a pizza is easy and after a few pages you will notice that....

Well, here we are, I tell you a secret;

When I'm in the kitchen I always follow two rules:

**Rule number 1** - simple things are the best ones

**Rule number 2** - good things have a enemy: the haste

Do you agree?

Yeah, I already knew it !

So what ?

**Follow me to the kitchen and let's start making you a pizza wizard!**

# What ingredients are needed to cook a pizza?

Do you remember the first rule? Simple things are the best ones!

So we need few ingredients, but good ones... let's have a look...

**For the compound we need:**

cake flour , dried yeast, sugar, water, table salt, olive oil

**The flavors are:**

Fresh mozzarella, peeled tomatoes (or chopped tomatoes), fresh basil, table salt, olive oil.

# What equipments are needed to cook a pizza?

A domestic mixer would be the best!

If you don't have it, no problem, we can knead the dough by hands, let's take;

Obviously, we also need an oven that can rich 240/250 grades.

# The recipe of the original home-made pizza Margherita

## For about 4 people

**Dough:**

500 grams of cake flour 6 grams of dried yeast 4 grams of sugar

300 grams of water 6 grams of salt

20 grams of olive oil

**Flavors:**

400 grams of tomatoes 4 grams of salt

6 grams of olive oil Fresh basil

300 grams of mozzarella

# How much dough should I put in a baking tin?

Are you ready to revise Math? Don't worry, it's very easy!

The right amount belongs to the kind of pizza you want to cook;

Do you want a thin pizza or an high pizza?

First, you have to count the baking tin's area (side x side : 2)

600 grams is the right amount of dough for a thin pizza

If you like high pizza instead, you have to add 20 % of dough;

720 grams is the right amount of dough for an high pizza.

To count the round baking tin's area we have to do: (radius x radius x 3,14 : 2)

is the Greek letter; it is a determined number that you always use, independently of the largeness of your baking tin.

353 grams is the right amount of dough for a thin pizza

If you want and high pizza instead,

you have to add 20% of dough and in this case we have to do:

423 grams is the right amount of dough for an high pizza.

# How to prepare an easy dough of a home-made pizza

Finally you will say: after all this time I got hungry!

Ok, let's do it now !

Let's start knead the dough by hands;

if you have a domestic mixer, you can go on by the same way , pouring in the same sequence the ingredients starting knead by the leaf and ending whit the hook (start with low speed end the baking

with the high one)

Let's go !

Pour the flour in a capacious bowl and add the dried yeast and the sugar .

Mix well these 3 ingredients by a spoon. Place the flour moving a little to the edges of the bowl, leaving an hole in the middle. Add water (room temperature) in the flour's middle, and start mixing with the spoon for few seconds, until the dough starts amalgamating.

Add salt, placing it on the dough. Continue kneading until it will be needed to knead by hands.

Knead by hands for about 5 minutes;

(i suggest you to do it in the bowl so you won't stain anything).

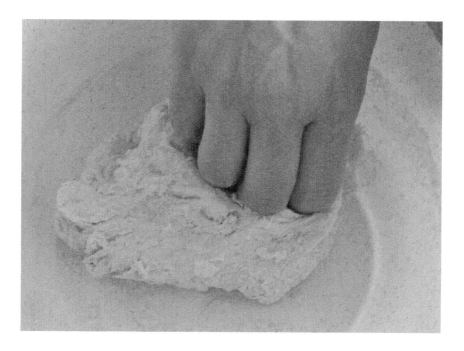

Does the dough looks a bit sticky?

It's a good thing; to have a great pizza we need a well hydrated dough,

not a marbled one!

Continue kneading

**without adding more flour,**

cause the dough

has to be quite moist.

After about 10 minutes of mixing the dough has taken shape very well .

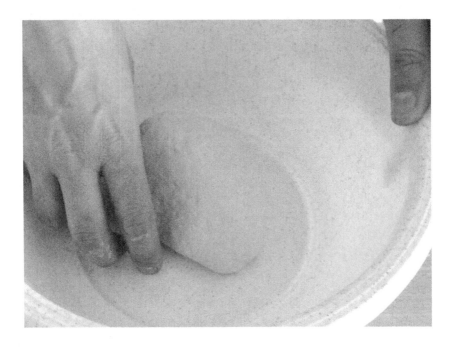

Now add olive oil and continue kneading for 5 minutes, doing an higher pressure to make it absorb.

At this point

the dough should dispose,

but don't you worry,

it will soon regroup!

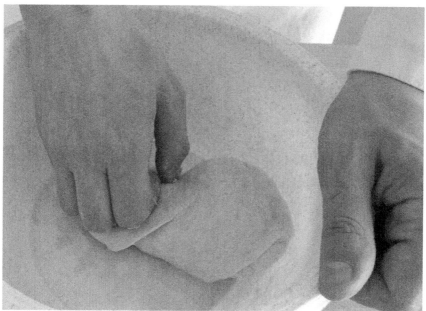

Continue kneading,

you are about to finish, there are 5 minutes left, hold on!

This is how it looks like after kneading for about

10 minutes.

Now that the dough is done, put a little olive oil in the middle of the bowl and place the dought on it.

If the dough is too big and it touches the bowl's edges, you have to brush them with olive oil.

**Finally the dough is done !**

Let it leaven for about 40/60 minutes .

or in another warm place,(in this case covered by a cloth, or by a cling film)

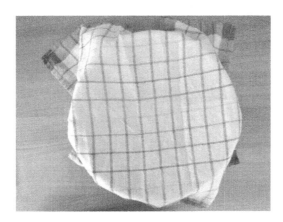

While the dough is leavening, let's prepare the tomatoes.

# The tomato's choice and the correct preparing

For a super delicious pizza, in perfect Italian style, you have to use peeled tomatoes, or chopped tomatoes

**Now:**

➡ **If you use chopped tomatoes;** you can easily place it in a bowl and add salt, olive oil and basil and mix with a spoon, crushing the bigger tomatoes pieces with a fork.

➡ **If you use peeled tomatoes instead:** you'll have to whisk it by yourself, and then spice it like described.

I suggest you to whisk it by vegetable mill, but if it's not possible, whisk it by a mixer (for a few seconds to

avoid that it gets too warm) with salt and basil (if you want),

(you will add it when you'll finish using the mixer).

# The mozzarella's choice and the correct preparing

The right choice:

for a great taste, use fiordilatte! About mozzarella, anyway,

to prepare a fantastic pizza, use a fresh one, in water.

Now that we know what kind of mozzarella we should use, let's start cutting it:

Cut the mozzarella in pieces of a cm per side

(we don't have to measure every piece but they must not be too small)

After having cutted it, put it in a colander, to let it loose serum.

# Roll out the pizza

Now that 60 minutes have passed, and the dough is well leaven,

let's roll out the pizza!

Take the baking tin and grease it with olive oil ;

(listen me, it's very important having a nonstick baking tin, in good

condition, otherwise the dough will stick..!)

At this point, take the boil with the dough, and with the oil that's placed on the edges, brush the dough on the surface.

This is a great help to brown the bottom of the pizza,

and to make sure it does not stick to the pan.

Well done !

Now reverse the bowl in the baking tin and let the dough slip.

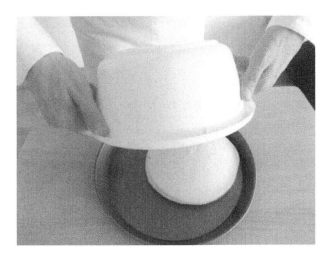

**Perfect !**

Now easily wet your hands ;

and start rolling out the pizza with your fingertips,

avoiding to stretch it. Massage it, doing pressure, going up and
then down

along the edges of the middle.

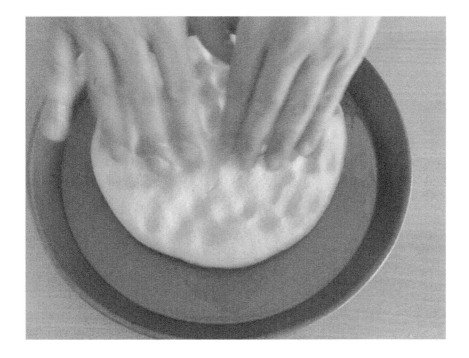

Repeat for a couple times until the dough is streched uniformly. (with hands wetted

to avoid the pizza will stick).

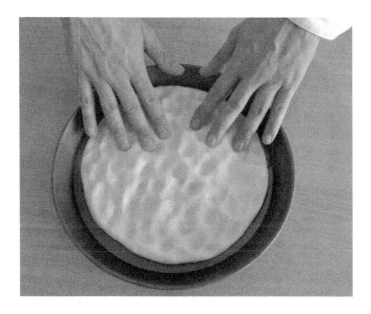

# Add flavors to the pizza:

Pour tomato on pizza with your hands (or with a spoon, if you want),

place it well, on the edges too, to avoid

that after the baking they get dried.

You can add a couple basil leaves and a little olive oil.

In this way the ingredients you add later, will remain "alive" and the pizza

will be delicious!

Now let's explain a thing; is this a pizza or a bun?
Now I'll say it, turn the page

and let's clear up!

# The difference between a pizza and a bun

With the word "pizza", we mean a dough that, after being rolled out and seasoned, needs to be putted in the oven without

waiting for another leaven;

**However, for an home-made work**, where we can have an oven that doesn't look like a professional oven like the ones we can find in a pizzeria,**I really suggest you to make the pizza leaven after have seasoned it with the tomato, for about 10/15 minutes,** before baking it;

trust me, the pizza will be a masterpiece!

Uhm, are we talking about masterpieces? ...........let's turn on the oven!

# The baking;
# the secret of a great pizza!

**The real secret of a great baking of the home-made pizza, is that the pizza has to be cooked for a few minutes, only with tomato and then with the other flavors!**

Well, now let's turn on the oven...get yourself ready for a dream with opened eyes !

Turn on the oven and let it reach 250 grades.

Put the pizza in the oven's lower part, and let

(if you have prepared the) for instead,

(if you have prepared and high pizza.)

Remove the pizza and then close immediately the oven and add other basil if you want, then the mozzarella and a little olive oil.

**Look out:**

Put the basil on the tomato;

it has to be on the mozzarella, otherwise it burns!

Now that the mozzarella is added, put the pizza in the oven,

End the baking after 5 minutes,

for the thin pizza, same for the high one.

**Remember; the baking has to be followed; every oven is different and the times of baking are always indicatives !**

When the baking ends,

take the pizza and add fresh basil. With a skimmer,

remove it from the baking tin and let it cool down for 3-4 minutes on a stainless steel grid

so that the air also passes from below.

Doing this way,

the pizza will not get wetted with its steam

and it will remain crunchy

on the outside and soft inside.

That's the hardest part......... waiting for when the pizza is ready !

# There's our pizza !

# Now... what do we do?

Everyone, come to the table!

Let's enjoy our pizza with our favorite drink...

Yeah, that's what I call such a beautiful life!

# Enjoy your meal

TSSSSSS, I'm going,  But wait... Let me say,

## CONGRATULATIONS!!

Now you're a pizza wizard and everytime you'll doing it, you'll see, it will always be good!

*Giuseppe Giovenco*

Giuseppe Giovenco

Printed in Great Britain
by Amazon

79760248R00031